The Invisible Musician

Poems by
Ray A. Young Bear

HOLY COW! PRESS
DULUTH, MINNESOTA 1990

Cover: Mesquakie Shoulder Bag, 1978, by Stella L. Young Bear

Photograph of Ray A. Young Bear by John Upah

First Printing, 1990

Library of Congress Cataloging-in-Publication Data

Bear, Ray A. Young
  The Invisible Musician
    p.   cm.

  1. Fox Indians—Poetry. I. Title
PS3575.0865I58   1989
811'.54—dc20   89-45544
ISBN 0-930100-32-8 (cloth)   CIP
ISBN 0-930100-33-6 (pbk.)

Publisher's Address: Distributor's Address:

Holy Cow! Press   The Talman Company, Inc.
Post Office Box 3170   150—Fifth Avenue
Mount Royal Station   New York, New York
Duluth, Minnesota 55803   10011

This project is supported by a grant from the National Endowment for the Arts in Washington, D.C., a Federal agency.

The Invisible Musician

Contents

To Stella L. Young Bear,
my deepest gratitude.

The Invisible Musician

The Significance of a Water Animal

Since then I was
the North.
Since then I was
the Northwind.
Since then I was nobody.
Since then I was alone.

The color of my black eyes
inside the color of King-
fisher's hunting eye
weakens me, but sunlight
glancing off the rocks
and vegetation strengthens me.
As my hands and fingertips
extend and meet,
they frame the serene
beauty of bubbles and grain —
once a summer rainpool.

A certain voice of *Reassurance*
tells me a story of a water animal
diving to make land available.
Next, from the Creator's
own heart and flesh
O *ki ma* was made:
the progeny of divine
leaders. And then
from the Red Earth
came the rest of us.

"To believe otherwise,"
as my grandmother tells me,
"or to simply be ignorant,
Belief and what we were given
to take care of,
is on the verge
of ending . . . "

The Personification of a Name

Our geodesic dome-shaped lodge
redirects the drifting snow.

Above us, through the momentary
skylight, an immature eagle
stops in its turbulent flight
to gaze into our woodland
sanctuary.

Easily outstared, we rest our eyes
on the bright floor. He reminds us
further of his presence through
the shadow movement of his wings:

Portrait of a hunter
during first blizzard.

Black Eagle Child.

The Language of Weather

The summer rain isn't here yet,
but I hear and see the approaching
shadow of its initial messenger:
Thunder.
The earth's bright horizon
sends a final sunbeam directly
toward me, skimming across the tops
of clouds and hilly woodland.
All in one moment, in spite
of my austerity, everything
is aligned: part-land, part-cloud,
part-sky, part-sun and part-self.
I am the only one to witness
this renascence.
Before darkness replaces the light
in my eyes, I meditate briefly
on the absence of religious
importunity; no acknowledgement
whatsoever for the Factors
which make my existence possible.
My parents, who are hurrying
to overturn the reddish-brown dirt
around the potato plants, begin to talk
above the rumbling din.
"Their mouths are opening.
See that everyone in the household
releases parts of ourselves
to our Grandfathers."
While raindrops begin to cool
my face and arms, lightning
breaks a faraway cottonwood
in half; small clouds of red
garden dust are kicked into
the frantic air by grasshoppers
in retreat.

I think of the time I stood
on this same spot years ago,
but it was under moonlight,
and I was watching this beautiful
electrical force dance above
another valley.
In the daylight distance,
a stray spirit whose guise
is a Whirlwind, spins and attempts
to communicate from its ethereal
loneliness.

The Last Time They Were Here

In between the deafening locust-shrill
on the apple tree, the locusts pause
at their own noise and then
to a silent signal they drop down
to another leaf or branch,
stopping when the chorus
starts again.

The last time they were here
this is what I remember:

I see my grandfather kneeling before
rolls of our delicately-tied belongings.
He instructs, "It will always be important
as you travel in life to tie protection
as I have just done."

As we move without him now, I think
about my belongings, spread apart
in three different houses. No matter
how powerful my sinew star-symbols
over my writings, they are defenseless
without my actual presence.

The Reason Why I Am Afraid
Even Though I Am a Fisherman

Who is there
to witness the ice
as it gradually forms itself
from the cold rock-hard banks
to the middle of the river?
Is the wind chill a factor?
Does the water at some point
negotiate and agree to stop
moving and become frozen?
When you do not know the answers
to these immediately you are afraid,
and to even think in this inquisitive
manner is contrary to the precept
that life is in everything.
Me, I am not a man;
I respect the river
for not knowing its secret,
for answers have nothing
to do with cause and occurence.
It doesn't matter how early
I wake to see the sun shine
through the ice-fishing hole;
only the ice along
with my foolishness
decides when
to break.

The Song Taught to Joseph

I was born unto this snowy-red earth
with the aura and name of the Black Lynx.
When we simply think of each other,
night begins. My twin the Heron
is on a perpetual flight northward,
familiarizing himself with the landscape
of Afterlife, but he never gets there . . .
because the Missouri River descends
from the Northern Plains
into the Morning Star.

One certain thing though,
he sings the song of the fish
below him in the mirror
of Milky Way.

It goes:

In this confrontation,
the gills of the predator
overtakes me in daylight near home;
in this confrontation,
he hinders my progress with a cloud of mud he stirs.
Crying, I ask that I not feel each painful part
he takes, at least not until I can grasp
in the darkness the entrance
of home.

From the Spotted Night

In the blizzard
while chopping wood
the mystical whistler
beckons my attention.
Once there were longhouses
here. A village.
In the abrupt spring floods
swimmers retrieved our belief.
So their spirit remains.
From the spotted night
distant jets transform
into fireflies who float
towards me like incandescent
snowflakes.
The leather shirt
which is suspended
on a wire hanger
above the bed's headboard
is humanless; yet when one
stands outside the house,
the strenuous sounds
of dressers and boxes
being moved can be heard.
We believe someone wears
the shirt and rearranges
the heavy furniture,
although nothing
is actually changed.
Unlike the Plains Indian shirts
which repelled lead bullets,
ricocheting from them
in fiery sparks,
this shirt is the means;
this shirt *is* the bullet.

All Star's Thanksgiving

1965

At midnight
when we finally signalled for
and received permission
to go outside and relieve
ourselves, I stepped off
the porch onto a steep cliff.
Immediately, I dropped
to the ground for fear
I would tumble down
the mountainside.
"Get up," said Facepaint,
the trickster who brought
me to his relative's *amanita*
congregation.
"There are no mountains
in the Midwest," he added.
Later, after he got me upright,
we went back inside.
Comforted by people,
I sat back against
the log cabin wall
and closed my watery eyes.
Suddenly, I was sitting on
a tropical beach with my legs
in the vibrant surf. In the breeze
I felt the sun's warmth. I became
sleepy, and when my head sank
into the wall, I woke up.
I soon discovered that
my left leg was missing.
I truly thought I had
sacrificed it as a brake
on the mountainside.

My frantic inquiry
made a spectacle until
an old man directly across
from me theorized "the leg"
probably became numb under
my weight. When I looked,
it was there. But the missing
leg dream was a minor problem
compared to the disconcertion
of thinking oneself in a state
of religious purpose: bilingual
songs and cigarette-smoking
constellations.

Eagle Crossing, July 1975

Without Selene
he didn't know what to do.
As was the case with his grandfather,
he felt no recourse but to start
a sculpture-mask,
hollowing out
the dish at first,
and then carving the face
of the Big Footed One,
Me ma ki ka ta ta.
He saw himself
as this reclusive entity,
confined to wait for
the glacier-aided breeze
of a summer night.
There were frequent
dreams that she would soon
return to caress the areas
where his human arms
and legs once were;
her perfumed fingers
would come through
the cottonwood mask
and touch his closed eyes.
To him, the summer was simply
the odor of accidentally burnt
skin, filtering like snake newborn
through the oven racks.
He sat before warm, uneaten
t.v. dinners, and he paid
little heed to self-collapsing
trash bags.
No longer could he
remember the details
of crisp frosted mornings

when he unerringly invited
names of both enemy
and relative into
his offering of flint chips
and shavings from a black
antelope tine. From a silver
Spanish lancepoint, which served
as the body of the feather-fringed
pipe—a symbol of epic campaigns
and Flag Wars—he smoked this mixture
along with Friesland tobacco, and he
thought of the mythical hot sun region
where the-people-who-pulled-up-their-
ladders lived. He saw himself
as a god-like antelope dodging
musket balls before his death.
The crudely-shaped star felt cool
on his chest: Religion & Broken
Hearts, he recited, somewhere
high above the earth's backbone
in the month of Thunder Moon.
Postcard from a suicidal year.

Three Poems

1979

1.

The high uncut grass was covered
with a cool sheen of dew.
Grasshoppers sat quietly
in the shadows—oblivious
to the fact that the price
of gasoline was the reason
for their August bed
and comfort.
The sun was beginning
to filter and mix into
the new green-colored forest,
all of which made for a ritualistic
morning.
There was never any indication
as to what made the Nicotines
decide to gather frogs
from their yard for bait.
First, the wife would merely
suggest the catching of *sha qwa me qwa*
when the humidity decreased,
how in the bank-pole evening
they would throw out their lines,
sensing by the firm splash
over the river's depth that they
were about, just by that sound
alone.
Unconsciously, the husband
would bring out the bait bucket.
Together they would talk,
reassuring each other if
they could find at least six frogs
before the sun fully rose,

tomorrow would mean fried flathead,
boiled potatoes, wild onions,
and Canadian ale.
Further, it would be an opportunity
to set aside portions of their catch
to supplicate *those who have passed,*
implanting within themselves this doubt
and reverence for existence.

2.

Everything is arranged for us
when we arrive in the small Norwegian town
for the poetry reading. To welcome us,
they release the Styrofoam snow,
and restaurants list the food
we like in their menus:
spaghetti for Selene
and chili for me.
Although we whisper
to each other as to what
we should drink, the waiter
with extraordinary hearing
orders milk and Pepsi from
a distance. On our drive
to the cliffs where the ancient
glaciers supposedly stopped,
we observe Caucasians who dress
and act like Indians: three middle-
aged men sit on a car hood and drink
their whiskey in public; an old lady
walks to town in a strong, even pace.
Jokingly, I sometimes tell friends
they have white opposites, but when
I actually meet mine, it isn't comical.

But through him, we are here.
Contrary to what is written
on the dust jacket of his poems,
I have never seen Mikhail B.
on or near the tribal settlement.
To say you are *a part* is no easy
matter. Before I question other
people's lives, there is my own
to consider. Together we read
from our work. I am sure the freshman
students do not understand my life
as easily as his. However, they are
amused at my ms. rejections from
elite east coast publications
(anything east of the Mississippi),
and why I am beyond the listless primitive
who tracks the extinct wolf.
After classes, a bearded professor
invites us to his country house —
a remodeled mental institute.
During lunch, adopted Chinese
children dash in and the professor's
wife plunges a spoon of peanut butter
into their mouths. I suddenly realize
when I touch the Chinese girl's
warped head that this place isn't real,
that it was arranged in haste.
The Martians are fascinated
by the cutbead barrettes
on my wife's hair and I am
puzzled why they have invited us.

3.

Before graph paper existed,
you planned the first series of geometric
communiques.
Although I can't decipher
the signals or the code,
I know from having seen computers
there is something reaching me.
The Czechoslovakian cutbeads which decorate
the barrettes in your hair
flash synchronously
by the candlelight: U.F.O.
I discuss the plight
of the grasshopper who had chosen
me the day previous (on my way
to the university) to oblige
his planned suicide by jumping
onto my path.
In Indian I told him:
It's simple to end yourself,
but me, I am in the human snowdrift already
in need of permanent shelter, simple income
and some excitement.
Venison takes the space in my freezer;
otherwise, I would take you there
as a favor to let you sleep until
the Iowa River freezes over and lower you
on hook in exchange for prehistoric-
looking fish.

Mesquakie Love Song

Ne to bwa ka na,
bya te na ma wi ko;
ne to bwa ka na,
bya te na ma wi ko;
ne to bwa ka na,
bya te na ma wi ko.

Ne a ta be swa
a ta ma
sha ske si a.

Ne to bwa ka na,
bya te na ma wi ko.

My pipe,
hand it over to me;
my pipe,
hand it over to me;
my pipe,
hand it over to me.

I shall light and inhale
tobacco
for the single woman.

My pipe,
hand it over to me.

Emily Dickinson, Bismarck

and the Roadrunner's Inquiry

I never thought for a moment
that it was simply an act of fondness
which prompted me to compose
and send these letters.
Surely into each I held
the same affection as when
we were together on a canoe
over Lake Agassiz in Manitoba,
paddling toward a moonlit fog
before we lost each other.

From this separation came
the Kingfisher, whose blue and white
colored bands on chest and neck
represent the lake-water and the fog.
But this insignia also stands
for permafrost and aridity:
two climate conditions
I could not live in.

It's necessary to keep your apparition
a secret: your bare shoulders,
your ruffled blouse, and the smooth
sounds of the violin you play
are the things which account
for this encomium for the Algonquin-
speaking goddess of beauty.

Like the caterpillar's toxin
that discourages predators,
I am addicted to food
which protects me,
camouflages me.
I would be out of place
in the tundra or desert,
hunting moose for its meat and hide,
tracking roadrunners for their feathers.

But our dialects are nearly the same!
Our Creation stories hopped out
from a nest of undigested bones,
overlooking the monolithic glaciers.
This is what we were supposed to have
seen before our glacial internment.
That time before the Missouri River
knew where to go.

My memory starts under the earth
where the Star-Descendant taught me
to place hot coals on my forearm.
"In the Afterlife, the scar tissue
will emit the glow of a firefly,
enabling one to expedite the rebirth
process. This light guides one's way
from Darkness."

The day I heard from you,
I accidently fell down the steps
of a steamboat and lost consciousness,
which was befitting because
there was little rationale
for the play (I had just watched
onboard) of a man who kept
trying to roll a stone uphill,
a stone which wanted to roll downhill.
I found myself whispering
"No business politicizing myth"
the moment I woke up.
Gradually, in the form of blood
words began to spill from
my injuries: Eagle feathers
1-2-3 & 4 on Pipestone.

I now keep vigil for silhouettes
of boats disappearing over
the arête horizon.
I keep seeing our correspondence
arrange itself chronologically,
only to set itself ablaze,
and the smoke turns to radiant
but stationary cloud-islands,
suspended on strings above
Mt. St. Helens, Mt. Hood
and Mt. Shasta: Sisters
of Apocalypse waiting
for Joseph's signal.
They tell me of your dissatisfaction
in my society where traffic signs
overshadow the philosophy
of being Insignificant.

It is no different
than living under a bridge in Texas
beside the Rio Grande.
Please accept advice from the blind
pigmentless Salamander
who considers his past an inurement.
"Perplexity should be expected,
especially when such a voyage
is imminent."

I want to keep you as the year
I first saw your tainted photograph,
preserved in an oval wooden frame
with thick convex glass,
opposite the introvert
you were supposed to be,
walking in from the rain,
a swan minus the rheumatism.

All of a sudden it is difficult
to draw and paint your face
with graphic clarity,
when the initial response is to alter
your age.
Automatically, the bright colors
of Chagall replace the intent.
When the Whirlwind returned
as a constellation,
we asked for cultural acquittance,
but when the reply appeared as herons
skimming along the updraft
of the homeland's ridge,
we asked again.
It was never appropriate.

We were disillusioned,
and our request became immune
to illness, misfortune and plain hate.
Or so we thought.

Contempt must have predetermined
our destiny.
To no avail I have attempted to
reconstruct the drifting halves
to side with me.
All that time and great waste.
Positive moon, negative sun.

Way before she began to blossom
into a flower capable of destroying
or healing, and even during times
she precariously engaged herself
to different visions,
I was already dependent upon her.
Whenever we were fortunate
to appear within each other's prisms,
studying and imploring our emissaries
beyond the stations
of our permanence,
I had no words to offer.

Mesmerized, she can only regret
and conform to the consequences
of an inebriate's rage
while I recede from her
a listless river
who would be glad
to cleanse and touch

the scar the third mutant-flower
made as it now burns and flourishes
in her arms.

I would go ahead and do this
without hint or indication
you would accept me,
                    Dear Emily.

The Suit of a Hand

He is finally asleep,
but first his coma sent the Mysterious Rat
who knocked and left scratch marks
on our door. We thought a cure was being
offered. But that same night,
as a result of our inability
to decipher the Rat's spelling,
a crane swerved above us
on the highway. We knew then daylight
had been ceased, that the Being of Fire
seen jumping from the wreckage
was death.

Shadows of past lives—
his mother, father—called him.
Even the Negative Parrot tried.
Death is lonely—a dangerous spring,
it must have planned on saying.
I now return for you . . .

But the Parrot was weightless;
it couldn't enter the hospital
to personally observe my relative's
demise. The Parrot's "soul" is stuck
in the entrance where electricity
combined with the weight of flesh
and blood only opens the second door:
I strangled the fluorescent green bird
in the glass enclosure before it had
a chance to revert to its original human
shape. Gita, the Danish nurse, in an ultra-
white uniform approached and screamed,
"What the hell are you doing?"

I mistook her as an evil accomplice
and threw the asphyxiated bird
to her.

I feel trapped: like The Incorporeal Hand
which wears the suit of a human hand,
punching out to us violently from inside
an empty grocery bag. The abundance of food —
fruits and meats — has no deterring effect.
No regard for the holidays. The whole thing
reminds me of an Alfred Hitchcock movie.
I taste the wind with my antennaes
and regress at the sound of a crow's
masculine howl.

The King Cobra as Political Assassin

May 30, 1981

About two miles east of here
near the Iowa River bottom
there is a swampy thicket and inlet
where deer, fox and eagles
seem to congregate every autumn
without fail.
When I am hunting there
I always think:
if I were an eagle
bored by the agricultural
monotony of Midwestern landscape,
I would stop, too.
This morning I dreamt
of a little-used road going
from an overlooking hill down
into their divine sanctuary.
I tried to drive through
thinking it was a short cut
towards tribal homeland,
but stopped after the automobile
tires sank into the moist earth.
I walked down the ravine and met
two adolescents and inquired
if the rest of the road was intact
or passable. A bit wary of me
they indicated that they didn't
know. A faceless companion
rolled down the car window
and spoke in Indian.
"Forget them! They shouldn't
be here, anyway."
I walked on. Further down
I met a minister and began
to chat with him about
the tranquil scenery,
how far the road extended

into the land founded
by the Boy-Chief in 1856.
(I avoided the personal
question of whether the dense
timber reminded him of South America.)
He turned and pointed with his black arm
to a deteriorating church mission
in a distant valley.
"Yes," I said. "The Founder's wish —
when he purchased this land —
was a simple one."
Soon, a hippie with an exotic snake
wrapped decoratively around
his bare arms and shoulders joined
our polite and trivial
conversation about directions.
As we were talking the hippie
released his hyperactive pet.
We watched it briefly as it slithered
over the willows. We did not think
too much of the snake until it slid
towards a nearby stream,
stopping and raising its beady-eyed
head intermittently, aware of prey.
Following it, we discovered what held
its attention: a much larger snake
was lying still and cooling itself
in the water. I told the hippie,
"You better call your pet."
With a calm face he said,
"I'm not worried; watch
the dance of hunting motions."
And we did.
The larger water snake recoiled
into its defensive stance

as the smaller slid into
the water. Before each came within
striking distance, the hunter-snake
struck. They splashed violently
against the rocks and branches.
Decapitated, the water snake's
muscled body became lax
in the sunlit current.
I thought about this scene today
and the events which led to it
many times over, analyzing its
discordant symbolism.
I finally concluded this dream
had nothing to do with would-be
assassins, cinema-child prostitutes,
political decision-makers or anything
tangible. In *Journal of a Woodland Indian*
I wrote:
"It was a prophetic yearning
for real estate and investments;
something else, entirely . . . "

A Drive to Lone Ranger

Everyone knows the Indian's existence is bleak.
In fact, there are people who have taken it upon
themselves to speak for us; to let the universe
know how we live, eat and think, but the Bumblebee —
an elder of the Black Eagle Child Nation —
thinks this sort of representation is repulsive.
This past winter, after our car conked out
in 80° below zero winds, we decided to pay him
our yearly visit. Although part of it was done
for amusement, we soon found out there were serious
things in life to consider. The poem which follows
was written without much revision. In fact, most
of it was composed in his earth lodge. I can still
remember the warmth of his antique woodstove,
as well as the silence after he shut off
his generator. He smiled at us as he accepted
a carton of Marlboro cigarettes.

For listening and instructional purposes,
the Bumblebee confesses that he sleeps
with earphones attached to his apian body.
"As the crisp December wind makes the constellations
more visible, so too, are the senses. Our vision
and hearing benefits from this natural
purification. Hence, the earphones."
In a lethargic tone someone offers
the standard "so they say" answer.
But the old man is unaffected,
and he continues to animate
what is in his Winter Mind.
"Ever since the Stabs Back clan
made the decision to accept education
for the tribal reserve in the late 1800s
there has always been an economic
depression. And now, when the very land

we stand on could reverse this congenital
inequity, the force which placed us here
seeks to take back this land with force
disguised as sympathy."
From communal weatherization
to peyote songs, regional and world
affairs, his bilingual eloquence
made topical events old news.
Every other topic a prophecy come true.

After an incident in the Badlands
(on a roadside town noted for its
commercialized springwater) when
cinder rocks had been deliberately
placed in his food — some of which
he had already ingested — he no longer
believes *trapping* is limited to his kind.
"I distrust capsules to begin with, and now
I am wary of cooks who are able to look out
at customers from their greasy kitchens.
But aspirins are my salvation. Rural
physicians refuse to prescribe codeine
and Valium on the premise *we* have no
reason to get headaches or depression."
We respond with an analogy:
if we were in Russia, the allotment
of vodka could not even begin to alleviate
our pain. Gravel is basically harmless,
but the message from the Badlands
restaurant is lucid.

Over pheasant omelettes and wine
he offers an explanation about his obsession
with technology.
"It may seem a contradiction,

but those cassette tapes on the wall
are the intellectual foundation
of my progeny."
Everyone laughs at the subliminal
connection to the earphones
and where they are placed,
breaking the tension.
We are accustomed
to his condescending attitude,
but underneath our Transformation Masks
we respect the old man, Bumblebee,
for he has retained the ability to understand
traditional precepts and myths. Moreover,
he understands the need to oppose
"outside" mining interests.

As he lights the candle on the mirrored
sconce, he translates our thoughts.
"Adjusting and manipulating
the strings and pulleys
of the exterior/interior masks
requires work at all levels.
The best test is the supernatural:
how to maintain calmness during its
manifestation; to witness and experience it
as it simply is, rather than camouflage it through
rational explanation."

In the gradual darkness our conversation
centers on Northern Lights:
celestial messengers in green atomic oxygen,
highlighted by red — the color of our impending
nuclear demise.
A hand-rolled cigarette begins
to glow from Bumblebee's lips.

Silhouetted against a white kitchen
cabinet, he rises from the sofa chair
and unfolds his transparent wings.
Just when we feel the motion of his wings
the candle goes out.

Before suggesting a drive in his pickup
to Lone Ranger to see the Helena Whiteskins
gamble in handgames with the Continental Dividers,
he reviews the strategy of the tripartite powers:
the Lynx claims Afghanistan and Poland;
the Serpent feels threatened and cannot
choose sides. Having ravaged what he
can't ravage anymore, the Eagle
becomes vulnerable. Once the Three
(volcanic) Sisters in California,
Oregon and Washington decide
to speak, the Missouri River
will reroute itself.
Satellites are taking photographs
of our sacred minerals from space,
revealing what we can't see but know
is there.
"In time we'll become prosperous,
or else we'll become martyrs
protecting the vast resources
of the Well-Off Man Mountains . . .
The force that placed us here
cannot be trusted."

The First Dimension of Skunk

It is the middle of October
and frosted leaves
continue to introduce
their descent as season
and self-commentary.
On the ground yellow-jacket
bees burrow themselves
into the windfall apples.
On the house the empty body shells
of locusts begin to rattle with
the plastic window covering
torn loose the night previous
in the first sudden gusts of wind.
South of the highway bridge
two extinct otters are seen
by Selene's father while
setting traps.
"Mates swimming;
streamlined and playing
games along the Iowa River."
In the midst of change
all it takes in one anachronism,
one otter whistle.

For us, it began with the healthy-
looking salamander who stopped our car.
So last night we stood in the cold
moonlight waiting for the black
coyote. No animal darted
from tree to tree, encircling us.
There was a time in an orange grove
next to the San Gabriel Mountains
when I was surrounded by nervous
coyotes who were aware
of the differences

between thunder
and an earth tremor.
Selene motioned for me to stand
still, and the moonlit foothills
of Claremont disappeared.
An owl began to laugh.
I remained quiet and obliged
her gesture not to mimic its laugh,
for fear we might accidently trigger
the supernatural deity it possesses
to break this barrier—
and once again find ourselves
observing a ball of fire
rise from an abandoned garden
which separates into four fireflies
who appear like four distant jets
coming into formation
momentarily
before changing into one intense
strobe light,
pulsating inside an apple tree,
impervious to hollow-point bullets,
admissions of poverty and car lights.

We stood without response
and other disconnected thoughts came.
From the overwhelming sound
of vehicles and farm machinery,
together with the putrid odor
of a beef slaughterhouse,
such anticipation
seemed inappropriate.
Whoever constructed
the two railroad tracks
and highways through Indian land

must have planned and known
that we would be reminded daily
of what is certainty.
In my dream the metal
bridge plays an essential part
and subsequent end of what
was intended to occur.
I would speak to the heavy
glass jar, telling it
the paper bullet
was useless underwater.

Three days ago, in the teeth
of Curly and Girl, a skunk
was held firmly and shook
until lifeless.
The first evening
we hear its final death call.
At the same hour the second night
we hear it again. The third night-
sound is more brave and deliberate;
it waits to blend with the horn
of an oncoming Northwestern train,
forcing us to step backward,
taking random shots at objects
crashing through the brush.

We have a theory that Destiny
was intercepted, that the Executioner
ran elsewhere for appeasement.
We also think the skunk's
companion returned on these nights
to mourn a loved one,
but all had to be deleted,
leaving us more confused.

Yesterday, we examined the dead
skunk and were surprised to find it
three times less the size I first
saw it with Mr. D.
My parents offered an explanation.
"A parrot or a pelican on their
migratory route."
With our surroundings
at someone else's disposal,
all we have are the embers
and sparks from our woodstove
and chimney: the fragrance
to thwart the supernatural.

Mesquakie Tribal Celebration Songs

Flag Song:

Ma ni ma wa wi ka
ta na se ki
ke ki we o ni.

This flag
shall wave
forever.

A qwi tta ka na qwa
ne ka ski te a te ki
tta ki a na to wa ta
ma ni ke ki we o ni

No, not ever
shall it be overtaken
by men of many languages—
this flag.

Veteran's Song:

Wa ta se a ki
wa tti na ni mi
ya qwi.

These veterans
are the reason we (are able to)
dance (in celebration).

Round Dance Song for Veterans:

Tte ma na
ne ma yo a
wa wo si ta
ma yo to ki

This German,
I made him cry.
His father
must cry now as well.

Wa ta se Na ka mo ni, Viet Nam Memorial

1982

Last night when the yellow moon
of November broke through the last line
of turbulent Midwestern clouds,
a lone frog, the same one
who probably announced
the premature spring floods,
attempted to sing.
Veterans' Day, and it was
sore throat weather.
In reality the invisible musician
reminded me of my own doubt.
The knowledge that my grandfathers
were singers as well as composers—
one of whom felt the simple utterance
of a vowel made for the start
of a melody—did not produce
the necessary memory or feeling
to make a *Wa ta se Na ka mo ni*,
Veterans' Song.
All I could think of
was the absence of my name
on a distant black rock.
Without this monument
I felt I would not be here.
For a moment I questioned
why I had to immerse myself
in country, controversy, and guilt;
but I wanted to honor them.
Surely, the song they presently
listened to along with my grandfathers
was the ethereal kind which did not stop.

Race of the Kingfishers: In Nuclear Winter

1.

Nobody on earth has a book of matches.
The German-silver tobacco box
and the optical burning lens
which has been built into its lid
is useless on gray blustery days.
For the moment, however, the mirrorlike
antique represents a star on the walnut
coffee table next to the iron striker,
flint and black antelope tine.
"This arrangement," notes
the elderly man named Bumblebee,
"is the tribal celestial system."
He illustrates this concept
through the quick sculpturing
of minature Sturgeon and Kingfisher
effigies in the frosted dirt.
I urge myself to pronounce
and memorize this sequence
correctly. *Should I ever see*
the real Night Sky:
The Child-Twin is trapped
between two of the brightest
stars in the Orion constellation,
and the child's earthly counterpart
is an air bubble, moving in accordance
to the pressure of our combined weight
beneath the clear river ice.

Stars have been hiding though,
and the eight snowdrift formations
cover the landscape without order.
I think of Polynesians who cannot
navigate in darkness over the ocean.

Startled by a rushing noise,
we look upward: lost seagulls
propel themselves against
the onslaught of snowflakes.

Unaffected by flood sounds
and ice jams, a lone frog—
the invisible musician—begins to emit
a low mournful song of tribute
to men-relatives whose names
are carved on a rock.
We understand
part of the song goes to men
who became an Indochina memory
after their return home.
Although they are gone,
they frequent our dreams:
two Bloody Mary drinks, a silk
navigator's scarf and golden
shoulder braids. On a concrete bridge
where giant frothy waves crash to an unseen
ocean, we honor them in the same
breath as the Trung Sisters.
This indefinite hour when
the river carries the wreath
northward—the wrong way.

2.

Above us, through the lodge portal,
the sun's double appears and causes
insects to release their numb bodies
from the ceiling into flight.
We question which myth foretold
of this neverending storm.

Through the thin wall, a voice
informs us we've lost controllable
fire. In a gesture made by thoughtless
men, we invite the voice to sit with us.
But when a child-entity enters our lodge,
wearing a perforated parka, we shield
our eyes from starlight coming through
clothes of poverty.

Each social order of the Locust
and Vulture worlds we inhabit
disagrees with our principal
belief. From each world we learn
wooden stakes cannot be twisted
to make our faces young. When
artificial intestines cease
to pulsate with the land
we will disappear again.

Motivated by tall, jagged mountains
encircled by clouds, eagles and pine
saplings, we try to make ourselves
credible to the Salamander
who was among the first
creatures.

If Paracelsus only knew . . .

3.

Outside in the wintry wind,
elegantly dressed women dance around us,
holding silver saxophones. They pretend
to smoke these instruments. Before
building up courage to step outside

and ask for a precious match
from the observers, I think
of Sherlock Holmes and his double-
brimmed hat, wondering whether
he could have solved the mystery
of the missing Night-Sky.
Upon my return, the old man
hands me a crumpled cigarette.
After a short pause for a light,
he takes a drag and talks in his smoke.
"Imported beer makes me philosophical. . . "
Later, in a demanding, raspy tone,
he asks if I have more canned beef
or Dutch beer. My wife, Selene, is offended,
but she shrugs it off. (Her eyes tell me
she knows something we don't.)

Pointing to the woman dancers,
our metamorphic guest narrates
the meaning of their intricate steps:
"In their Kingfisher costumes, they will
adjust with strings and pulleys the bird's
facial expressions while reciting complex
prose from within. Their purpose is
to apprise us of the Aurora Borealis,
and how such lights will bring
the true end." During a break
before the race of these spirits,
several dance attendants walked
up to the birds and laid out
blankets beside them, displaying
mementoes from previous Flag Wars.
"Simply by inhaling their air
with imaginary straws," whispers
our guest, "we derive good luck."

4.

Rappeling on their life strings,
caterpillars slowly stream down
from the intersecting lodge poles.
Without the presence of a healthy
cooking flame, they descend into
cool ashes. As fiery sparks begin
to materialize on an overturned skillet,
the caterpillars stop.
I resolve that wounded men
are being retrieved or dug out
somewhere in the Persian terrain.

Acknowledging the need for conflict,
and citing the story where the Heron
flew over Montana, following
the Missouri River,
familiarizing itself
with the land of Afterlife,
I rise from my chair and walk
towards the octagon drum.
Before I have a chance
to tighten the glossy drumhide
with the antelope tine,
I find myself standing in blue
tropical water. Like an infant
I try to maintain my stance,
but a huge fish swirls by,
sending a wave through
my tremulous body.

5.

Before our elderly guest left,
content that *Race of the Kingfishers*
coincided with his goal, he knelt
on the floor again and doubled
his right hand into a fist as if
he was about to send forth a marble.
Instead, he drew diagrams of the earth's
interior with lines of black sand.

As the blizzard changed into harmless clumps
of wet snow, the candlelight became steady
and bright. I thought about a painting
I had stored long ago: in dynamic
poster colors, an individual
with ironed Levis and cowboy boots
sits in a jetseat with his brown
crooked hand clutching a plastic
cocktail glass, and the window beside
him shows snowcapped mountains
with a city below them protruding
from mud. (I knew then that our
beginning was to be our end.)
I found and unwrapped the painting,
wiped the grime from the acetate cover
and read its title: *Indian Subject Asleep
On Flight 544 After Lecture On Tribal
Prophecy.*

6.

The next day when I met him
on the community's drift-covered road,
he explained his temperament was a result
of marital concerns. I said it made
no difference to my esteem, that Selene
knew all the facts. Afterwards, he showed
me his Czech cutbead buckle:
a moon of half-green and half-red beads
divided by a single horizontal line
of pearl beads. "It looks pretty good,"
I said. "A simple idea," he replied,
"but they are colors of sanctity."
I continued my walk, feeling glad
alcohol had not ruined my day.
Or his. "By the way," he said
sternly after we had walked
a few paces from each other
like chivalrous foes,
"you have a bug in your ear!"
In my heart I thought:
Why would anyone want me
under surveillance?
But my left ear had been humming.
When I turned around, three conspicuous men
with recording apparatus and earphones
tried to act as if they couldn't hear me.
In their pretense to walk into the snow-
blind, they stumbled when I spoke
to them.

Nothing Could Take Away
the Bear-King's Image

At first I thought I would feel
guilty in not missing you,
that despite its unfortunate
occurrence,
I would see you again
(exactly the way you were
before a hunter's arrow
glanced off some willows —
lodging near the pulsating song
of the Red Earth heart)
either here,
or towards that memorable direction
near the oily air of Los Angeles
where once a Zuni Indian companion
peered into a telescope aimed
at the Orion constellation:
"These three faint stars
are known for their alignment
rather than by four
of the bright stars which
frame them."

While we were sitting
on a manicured knoll
positioned above a Greek theatre,
we heard the distant skirling
sound
of Scottish bagpipes
coming through the eucalyptus trees.
We went to them, and there,
the astronomer-physicist
invited us to share his interest
in the night skies he was playing for.
He told a story of this Greek hunter
composed of stars;

the "Three-Stars-In-A-Row"
were his belt.
"I think that's me, grandfather,"
responded my Zuni companion,
"but I will believe you more
if you sell us your Scotch whiskey —
and consider the magnitude of my belief
if I told you the bubbles of my Creator's
saliva made the stars, grandson."
"Grandfather? Grandson? In the same
sentence? I am not related to you
in any way!" demurred the scholarly man.
The two Hispanics, Sergio & Camacho,
who were with us reaffirmed the Zuni's
request by bumping the academician
with their expanded chests.
"Grandfather, Grandson,"
they repeated.
Later, with erratic wind-notes
and chinking necklace shells,
my companion tripped and fell on
the professor's bagpipes
as he was completing
his third revolution
around the observatory.
He rolled down the sandy incline
breaking the instrument
into several pieces.
Suddenly, the professor's eyes
possessed a wild gleam,
a distant fire we hadn't seen before;
a nebula of sorts.
He knelt next to the dead instrument
and began to weep.
"My dear chanter! My drone!"

Like gentlemen, Sergio & Camacho
offered to pay for the irreplacable
antique parts, but it was too late.
We left (no, we fled from)
the observatory.

Back at the Greek theatre,
we found solace by the singing
of round and grass dance songs
with three Caucasians:
one jeweler, one ROTC student
and one KSPC disc jockey,
until we were greeted
by Sioux voices from the dark.
There was immediate silence,
and then the Sioux National Anthem:
"The United States flag will stand forever.
As long as it stands the people will live
and grow; therefore, I am doing this
say the Indian soldier boys."
The radio announcer advised us
the voice was amplified,
possibly by a handheld system.
Pretty soon, we were surrounded
by figures wearing bronze helmets.
The jeweler whispered to us.
"They look like Mudheads with metallic paint."
The military student observed and commented
on their evenly-spaced formation.
Several descended the stone steps
and their boot heels echoed
onto the stage.
When they got close
with their glistening visors,
nightsticks and badges,

we were bewildered.
The police officer explained
that he was a boy scout leader
and learning Siouan was essential.
"Would you boys consider singing
for our troop in Pomona?"
he queried before stating
the purpose of his visit.
"What disturbance?" we asked
in regard to bagpipes and walked back
to our individual dormitory rooms.
We called each other on the phone,
laughing at times, exchanging crazy
warhoops in a warm California night;
that ancient but comical time and place
where we hypothesized the draft
which lifted Marilyn Monroe's dress
came from the San Andreas Fault.
When it shifted, Orozco's murals
in Frary Hall actually moved,
responding to the land wave
and the force of the Pacific Ocean.

We are endless like the Central Plains
breeze in winter which makes the brittle
oak leaves whisper in unison of this
ethereal confidence.
Nothing could take away
the Bear-King's own image
who is human and walks.
There remains a bottle of champagne
beside the charred concrete block;
the half-smoked cigarette
of cornhusk and Prince Albert tobacco
which was propped next

to the green bottle
has disappeared
in the snowdrift.

The Spearbow Priest hasn't been summoned.
In the tribal gymnasium, exercise
equipment is marked by the greasy
handprints of a phantom infant.
The caretaker's two bows
and their arrows lie unpropelled.
The crooked snakelike arm doesn't
have the strength to draw back
the taut string, which would
have triggered an old-time
message to the brain.
On top of a moonlit hill
stands a boy whose lithe body
has been painted black
with numerous light-blue spots.
He signals us to follow him,
and he lights small fires
along the way.
Inside the earth-mound,
a small man in a bright-red headband
places an arrow in the bowstring
of his left hand which is bent
like a bow.
He explains the meaning
of the arrow's crest.
"From the birds the bison dreams about.
This shaft of wood tipped with sharpened flint,
together with the wolfskin draped over the hunter
crouching low against the salty earth . . . "

Nineteen Eighty Three

1.

It is January—
and simply because
the rain failed to change
into snow
the quiet river
has risen to flood stage.
Half-frozen rainwater
fills into a nearby pond
where once the sound
of frogs, crickets,
mosquitoes and birds
permeated the humid
summer night:
narcosis through
the sound of an open
window. Tomorrow
young children will
pretend to skate
over the thick pond ice,
but each day their figures
will slowly descend
into the ground,
reminding us
of mythical Rolling
Heads playing hockey.
The rainwater will evaporate
and ice will succumb
to the daily game.
Winter's indecision
makes us feel safe.
An elder, however,
would say "You're
basically unprepared."

No matter how *balanced*
one's mentality,
one's physicality.

2.

The gentle appearance
of the Female Death Light
from Wisconsin
takes place
in the center
of a soybean field.
Two times, a slow fire.
Inside the hollow wall
a mouse takes a chance
during our rumination
to weep like a human.
Throughout the neighborhood
the four-legged sentinels,
especially the all-white ones,
signal each other of this
Incongruity: a shadow
of an unknown tall being
stands in the flash
of lightning.

Cool Places of Transformation

Due to the flood-level force
of the Wapsipinicon River
each grain of sand
which has been loosened
from the radiant bone-white
beach, tumbles and disappears
into the swift, opaque undercurrent.
Slowly, in my desire for sleep,
I envision myself as this crescent-
shaped beach, alive but pensive,
feeling acquiescence as my senses
are gradually being divided,
examined, and swept away
by images of abandon and dream:

One of my ears detaches itself
from me and bounces along the river
floor and chooses wisely to ignore
pleas from the delicate sense
of *thought* lodged in the tan rocks
of a catfish sanctuary.
Both of my hands are able
to stop themselves in spite
of their inability to discern
exactly where assistance is needed.
Emulating the badger, my nose
burrows into the silt for no
reason. Although one of my eyes
knows from experience that long,
ominous shadows represent cool places
of transformation, its brother-eye
chooses to enter a desolate checker-
board alley (like the kind in a De
Chirico painting) and extricate

the deity who sacrificed its once
eagle beauty to shape earth's landscape.

Suddenly, after clouds of mud
and silt have been replaced
by the aroma of spearmint,
the senses form themselves
into a vulture who surveys
the mountains and glaciers
of Greenland, reliving their
painful Creation.

Moments later, I awaken
to the faint sounds of a mosquito
in ascent, escaping after it has drawn
metal-tasting blood from my chest
with a horn. On the mule deer hide
of an octagon drum, I see four
killer whales suspended
in the watery sunlight.
I feel loss in being neither
winged or aquatic creature.
Somewhere in the sky's glare,
mosquitoes will gather in clans
for a feast, and someone will rationalize
a greater entity could have done worse,
"such as the bluejay," wounding me
without ceremony . . .

Three Views of a Northern Pike

With a small round mirror
submerged upright
in an olive-green basin
of cool pumpwater,
I am hoping through
subtle maneuver
of this "true picture"
that the young Northern Pike,
held captive, will see
its majestic self
and therefore adduce
that the stagnant pool
(where I seined it)
would have evaporated
or become congested
with autumn leaves,
anyway.

During night or dawn,
in a flight of acceptance,
this fish will consider
the ebony cricket.
If it should eat something,
a leg or antenna,
or acknowledge itself,
my presence,
through fin flutter,
the thought of a four foot
forty-five pound predator
encircling us
in an aquarium
built between
the library shelves
will transform to love
and commitment.

Stationary, the pike hovers
before its prehistoric reflection;
its feathery rainbow-fringed gills
pulsating more evenly.
Soon, a large spot similiar
to a Union Jack flag
appears underneath its lucid skin:
I see the fish as a British Harrier jet.

As I take notes and sketch
the various perspectives
of clupeiforme, Woodland Indian
and convex mirror,
my eyes cannot shake
the transparent effect of water.
For a moment, I believe
it is a sanctimonious sign,
warning me.

Later, my respect is overruled
by an old time cerebral message:
should the fish be inverted
in the morning,
struggling to hold
its life,
I cannot keep it;
should it die before
reaching the river rapids,
I must use it as a lure.

Debut of the Woodland Drum

At the place
where Midwestern glaciers
supposedly came to a stop,
having created the last
buttes and stone cliffs
along the Mississippi
(which would one day remind
extraterrestials of home planet
and thus establish a colony
in the name of Scandanavia),
we listened to Debra Harry
of Blondie sing ATOMIC
four hours from Oneida,
Wisconsin.

A Woman's Name Is In The Second Verse:

Earthquakes and Parallels

In the dream before I noticed the predawn thunder
was actually an earth tremor, Lillian Nicotine
of Pinelodge Lake, resplendent in her purple
silk blouse and skirt, came up to me
and whispered unfamiliar pedagogical terms
in a Canadian dialect. (I knew it was half
in reference to a question made sixteen years
previous at the "54th Parallel" conference
on Algonquin linguistics.) Overtaken by memory
of her beauty, it took a few moments before
I fully understood what she was saying.
"Did you hear that?" she asked in alarm
as lightning began to flash through low clouds.
"The static in His PA system is merely thunder—
a signal that a song more powerful than the hymn
of angels is forthcoming."

When the thunder stopped, a song in supernatural
wattage began. It came down in falsetto,
reciting words of beauty, of totality,
of purpose. *"Ne ke ta ke be na,*
ne ke ta ke be na ma ni na ka mo ni. Wa ba to shi
me to se ne ni wa a na a ka wa ni!
We will throw it out, we will throw out
this song. Show the people your dancing ability!"
Although I believed the source was sacred,
I recognized the voice of Maker belonged
to Alfred Potato, a mortal. (It almost occured
to me then that the last time I saw Lillian,
a Middle Eastern lover had been too liberal
with his fists on her body, that I had even paid
her a visit: a fool with new flowers in hand,
lamenting her bruised body at the PHS Hospital
on St. Michael's Road. But the thought dissipated.)
The Maker's voice is like any human voice,

I said to myself. Like Alfred's. Twice my eyes
clouded. Hector and Sam Reveres Nothing—
victims of Indochina after the fact.
They were the only ones who could dance
for Earth.

Lillian placed her cool palm over my mouth
and said I should not inquire, offer explanations
or formulate a theory about the clear, wavering
voice that travelled over the landscape. I looked
at her beautifully slanted eyes in the lightning.
The infant-like skin on her nose was almost
transparent. She held on to my arm
and intentionally brushed her soft breasts
against my elbow. Her faint perfume intensified
my brain-induced paralysis.

After we walked in the opposite direction
of the cloudburst, we entered a green valley
lit by the summer sun. Squinting, we looked
at each other to reaffirm our pact, but we
had to turn around, pause, and marvel
at the point where the wall of dark rain
divided the region in two like a security light
defining ownership in a quiet rural evening.

To the north, a stone hill with terraces
delivered springwater into a small pond
filled with young walleye and pike fish
whose shiny gills pulsated in contentment
over the volcanic sand. To the south,
a row of apple trees stood under the fervent
attention of yellow jacket bees. When the first
minor tremor loosened and sent clumps of creosote
down the stovepipe, I saw Cody, the coyote-dog,

alive again, chasing grasshoppers and kicking
rocks over a dirt road. Next, thinking
I was in the path of mortar shell-fire,
I had to cringe under a star blanket
when the second landwave banged the stovepipe
inside the brick chimney. The third quake
shattered glass in the frames of doors
and windows. But the fourth — the fourth
broke the earth open.

The dormitory building I slept in named Smiley
toppled over the white Porsche that would have taken
me to LAX. *Plum blossom witchcraft*, I thought
the moment I heard listening devices coming down
through the twisted water pipes and tennis court
concrete. I woke up and realized the "Throw Out Song"
was the Maker's own summation of life that should
have been. Through the dark, inverted mass
a voice spoke out: "Is anybody down there?
If you are, call out and we will try to locate you.
Any sound you are able to make will help us."
There was a click and then silence.
I wanted to respond terribly, but the thick
bloodclot in my nose and mouth, along with intense
chest pain prevented it.

From somewhere below where I was suspended
a cry came out. "Oh God, please help me!"
It was the Caucasian who lived across the hall;
I recognized his slightly effeminate voice
from the rappeling practice he did with club
members from floor to floor in Smiley.
Although part of the cast iron railing,
which once held the mountain climbers' ropes
and clamps, was now embedded in my chest,

my heart continued to work. As the weight
of the earth shifted above me, I could feel
the stairway railings grind into the plaster
behind me. I saw myself as a spear-impaled fish
unable to move as the wooden pole and barbed tines
pushed me deeper into the silt and mud
for good measure.

Mesquakie Love Song

Ne qwi na ta wa na be na so
a ka me a ki
a ki wi ne o na ni

Ka na i skwa ke wa ba mo ni
ke wa wa-wa wa sa na ma wi no
ke wi a wa ni.

I would like to be taken (romantically)
in the distant forest
where I have been seeing you.

At least with your mirror
reflect, reflect for me
where you are.

Green Threatening Clouds

"Paint these green threatening clouds
a rose color," said Elvia near my shoulder.
"I mean around the fluffy sides to at least
give credence to these ceramic-looking pitchers
and their red corrugated brims. And how will you
convey the phenomena of luminous mountain plants
when they're nocturnal?"
She had two good points as far
as biology and the dispersal of colors
was concerned, but I was debating where
to hang the pitchers whose poisonous
contents, if consumed, would make this
jungle a lovely place to close one's eyes
in permanence and see that far-ahead time
when gravity-wise hawks would splinter
my hip bone against a mountainside
repeatedly for marrow access,
a time in respect when young bull
elks would nudge their antlers against
my half-submerged and decayed antlers
in the tundra, a time when my arctic
shadow would claim pieces of ice
as descendants and incubate them,
arguing with any penguin over
their ownership . . .

Outside, a Midwestern cardinal hovered
under the roof of my parent's prayer lodge
and delicately manuveured itself to the tip
of an icicle for a nonexistent drop of water.
In the snow-covered garden, a bluejay
disappeared into a brittle corn husk
and gave it momentary life, but none
was received from a dance made from
hunger. (Here we cannot migrate

to low altitude for tropical weather
and abundant food. Instead, like cultures
who wait for their savior, we wait for
a young man who has a neverending source
of food in his Magic Tablecloth.)
In our efforts to help the hungry birds,
we impale a slice of bread on a treelimb,
but it freezes and becomes a violent wind
sculpture. At thirteen below zero, a poorly
clothed child walks by with a lonely sled
in hand.

And then Elvia began talking about Saskatchewan.
"I dreamt of a large green eagle, and it was
speaking to me in French. I understood that
the eagle was an elder, who had flown *down*
in response to a song when a person is allowed
to leave its body."
"Does such a song exist?" I questioned.
"Of course," she replied. "Green. Such an
important color."

My Grandmother's Words (and Mine)
on the Last Spring Blizzard

The snow has fallen in variations.
Each variation has a meaning
which goes back to our *Creation*.
This morning, for instance,
branches broke under
the wet snow's weight.

Last night, in the snowstorm,
anyone could've gotten lost.

Such was the time before
our moment when the Good
eluded Evil . . .

(Despite a winter of doubt,
I owe my existence to the ally
who now rests on the ground outside
with *His* brilliant white blanket
covering the green grass-shoots
of another year.)

If the Word for Whale is Right

The old tribal messenger
whose grass-legbands
glided silently over
the sparse woodland
and prairie
began to sense
snowflakes landing
on his face.
He momentarily broke
from his stride,
but resumed it after
the realization that snow
was an ally:
a testimonial
opposite from
the fog.

Inspired by his commitment
to keep following
an invisible trail,
impervious to weather
and obstacle,
he wanted to compose
a song for his mentor
No no ke, Hummingbird,
whose rapid wings
fanned rocks, thorns
and branches aside
in front of him.

When the cold waters
of the Mississippi River
came up to his neck,
he listened to
the frenetic drumming

of his heart and lungs,
and then determined how
the song should go,
combining tune, lyric,
breath and situation
together.

"This very moment and ever since
my investiture as a divine runner,
I think of your help."

As he attempted to swim around
dangerous blocks of drifting ice,
he noticed the dark fins of *Me tti na me*
parallel to him,
silhouetted against a sandy beach.
Right away he thought:
A song for him, too!

Of course, a century later
his idyllic grandchildren
(while listening to their elders
sing inside the geodesic
dome-shaped lodge)
would fail to associate
or understand
the archaic term
for the nonexistent
whale.

Three Translated Poems for October

Old woman, I hope that at least
you will watch me in the future
when I am an elderly man —
so my baggy clothes
do not catch fire
when I socialize
with the young people
as they stand around
the campfire intoxicated.
Of course, I will tell them
worldly things.

$/\ /\ /$

Now that the autumn season
has started, one suddenly
realizes the act of living
goes fast.
Sometimes the spring
is that way too:
the green so quick.
Thirty-two years of age I am.
Box elder leaves are being shaken
by the cold rain and wind.
In the tree's nakedness
there stands a man,
visible.

$/\ /\ /$

Although there is yet
a lot of things to do,
surprisingly, I have this urge
to go fishing.
They say the whites

in town will pay
one hundred dollars
to whoever catches
the largest channel catfish
or flathead.
You know I like to fish.
We could invite and feed
lots of friends.
Plus, purchase
a cast iron woodstove
since the business committee
has ignored our weatherization
application, but Bingo
is on the agenda.

Journal Entry, November 12, 1960

Fred Bloodclot Red's Song to be Used
in the Spring for the Long, Narrow Fish
Who is Also an Eagle:

"I hide the two suns
from striking my face,
but I feel their warmth
equally on my palm.

They are brothers:
one born from water (and
related to the trapped
bubble under the ice),
the other sky . . .

In the shadow
made from my hand,
I feel their warmth
equally."

The Black Antelope Tine

When Lucretia Rude Youth took out her childhood
mementoes from the sewing box and placed them
carefully over the table, the kitchen air,
although imperceptible at first, became cooler
than the high waters that drove us to her house
for shelter. To perhaps conceal this change,
venison and coffee had been prepared —
our arrival anticipated.

The meal's warmth made me think of turtles
basking on peeled logs over the tribal dam.
That was the last day I was comfortable
before rains filled the lowlands.
We were going to stay, explained
the victims in us . . . But any plan
of escape, interjected Cree, is acceptance
of danger by morning. Which was true.
The flood history of the Swan Root
was depicted on her face. As a girl,
she said, I dove for *e si wa wa na ni*,
clam eggs or pearls. We listened, but
something was amiss.

Was it the night? Or was it the finely-
clothed figurines whose plaid material
resembled shirts we used to wear?
Did our frightened eyes reflect like
marble stars in the searchlights
of supernatural hunters?

Jesus, I once dreamt of doll-sized
human beings — six intoxicated dwarfs
who asked to be rolled together in a towel.
Put us in a trash can, they pleaded,
before we get arrested. They eventually

suffocated because I forgot to pick them up.
And now, here they were in the form of antique
toys. An alcohol-related tragedy.

Cree tried to keep our attention on Philippine
coins, old wax seals and war photographs,
but I was soon conscious of another strength —
cool and invisible — emanating from a cast iron
toy kettle. Her narrations about the deformed
pearl hunter became inaudible as autumn rain
exploded on the roof, sending slivers of light
out into the yard. Sleet. *There was this kind
of power once: tribal celebration dancers
flashed their sequins under the nightlights
and the ground bloated beneath their feet
until we all stood on what seemed a little
earth. We attempted to balance on its
curvature. Yet the dancers danced when
regalias alone could have disabled anyone.
Sharp triangles of bone in the heel and instep.
Roots to combat sorcery.*

Every article in Cree's kitchen,
including the woodstove and Selene's face,
was concentric. A slice of French bread
levitated over my palm. Beside two figurines
from the morning of forgotten dwarfs,
the odious mass of a Spanish galleon
broke through the toy kettle and hovered
under the ceiling. It was the same ship
whose ochre clouds held me down as a child
near death.

I found myself in the arms of my elderly father.
He was taking me to Well-Off Man's gathering
where I would soon be spoon-fed with *amanita* tea
to subdue my seizures. I knew all of this
and I wanted to say so. When we entered
the canvas and tin-covered lodge,
Calvin Star, the appointed drum-maker,
was winding a thin rope around the tripod
legs of an overturned kettle. In his delicate
but rapid hands, the black antelope tine
which would be used to tighten and tune
the drum sparkled in the kerosene lamp's
bronze light.

Quail and His Role in Agriculture

"Now it's here
that time which
was once forthcoming
for us to remember
our older/younger brother
Quail," was how I composed
a song for John Louis.
Though I had very little
to do with him socially
or the family way,
ever since my cousin
acknowledged his unrequited
love fifteen years ago,
I thought it befitting
to present this song
to him before the next
memorial.

As I began to drum on the car's
dashboard with my fingers,
several horticulturalists
who were waiting their turn
at the Tastee Freez line
looked my way. Their clothes
were resplendent: bright baseball
caps with fertilizer logos,
ironed overalls, and new workshirts;
but their faces were tired and expression-
less. With the constant drone of harvesting
machinery in their ears, they probably
thought the tapping was yet another
mechanical trouble to contend with,
for they were the only ones to turn
their heads. The rest just wanted
to order.

It was a hot September day, and we
had all stopped to have strawberry
sundaes: I, to celebrate my song;
and they, to soothe the grain and dust
in their throats. Midwesterners, all,
standing in the monolithic shadow
of a hydraulic platform, which lifted
the semi-truck's cab to the sky
to violently shake and dislodge
its cargo of yellow corn—
the historic sustenance
which was now to some
a symbol of abject poverty.
For others, like myself and all
my grandfathers before me, it continues
to be a transmitter of prayer.
Beautiful yellow corn . . .

Colleen's Faith

Colleen sweeps the floor
carefully and rearranges
the furniture as if guests
were expected. The crooked
branch, however, which measures
the river's depth in the yard
is an unerring reminder that
the earth's cool and dank
breeze is intended for us
alone. Every time we begin
to forget this ominous fact,
a strong, deliberate current
shakes and momentarily drowns
a row of berry bushes. For
the sixth night, the reflection
of our houselights will shimmer
against the land's distant
circumference. With the community's
great "registered" cottonwood
smoldering under an overcast sky,
no one will believe we are here
in the middle and deepest part
of the flood. On the sandy rapids
over the gravel road, old men
who have kept a day-long vigil
for black, ribbon-like forms
of leeches have gone home
to count their bait earnings,
leaving behind them the incessant
laughs of children who contradict
our plight as they swim like
strong carp over the hidden
culvert's upsurge of brown
water.

Fred Bloodclot Red's Composition:

For Use on the Third Night of Footsteps

The lower protruding jaw
of the Eagle-Fish is translucent.
This nightmare is the first thing
we see swimming warily around
the moss-covered stone bend
of a deep, clear river.

We cannot remain as silent
as the Blessing Constellations;
in haste, I instruct you to say
to yourself for Him: Father,
for the reason you are part-
water, part-sky, I am still
the trapped bubble under
the ice.

And still, I have not abused
anyone vocally or physically,
nor have I thought ill-will
to relative and friend. That
I will confess to anyone . . .

The cigarette you smoke,
which lingers in the oak
treetops above my room,
is the same brand as mine.

Always is He Criticized

There was this dance procession
I was a part of, and we were all males
following one another, demonstrating
our place in Black Eagle Child society
with flexed chest muscles and clenched fists.
(I later thought this image a cultural
paradox when some of us were supported
on income made by women. We were still
warlike but perennially unemployed.)
We were singing an energetic, non-
religious song, but we gave it
reverence as if it were one,
admonishing anyone who forgot
such compositions could not
have been made by humans.
The leader started the loud
repetitive verse and we quickly
joined in with voices amplified
by mountainous terrain. "Always
is he criticized, always is he
criticized — in the manner of a pig
I dance."

On our blistered hands and knees
we crawled up the difficult mountainside.
Sometimes we depended on the heart's blissful
intonation for dreams when powdery
snow incapacitated our bodies.
As the blizzard left for earth,
we saw the still, inflated corpses
of those who succumbed to His domain.
At one point, perhaps in a moment
of fatigue, I looked down the valley
and was amazed how far we had climbed,
singing the same song.

By nightfall I was still struggling
to keep up with the dance, and several
layers of ice and snow clung to my
chilled face like an Albino Mask.
Suddenly, up ahead past the Torn
Blanket faction, the leader said something
in reference to the one flashlight we had
and the loud breathing nearby. A dim beam
was directed to a large, lumbering shadow.
And here, whether it was part of the dance
or actual fear, we cringed at the sight
of our cousin who was outfitted in a loose,
oversized bear suit. He snarled and moved
about in anger. What he didn't realize
was that a real grizzly bear was standing
beside him, foaming at the mouth. Our cousin
couldn't hear, see or feel the giant bear's
presence. But he did wince in pain as the bear
drove an arrow into his ribs. Fred Bloodclot Red
was suspended on the wooden suit support like
a crucifix.

In half-delirium and half-sleep
I thought I heard new cowboy boots
being test-walked over the thin
floor boards of our trailer.
"For New England," Fred had joked
before his demise. As a lifetime
resident of Carson Red Hat Reserve
whose sole highlight would have been
this one lecture on tribal prophecy
at Cambridge, he was embarassed
for being dependent on his grandmother
for footwear. But he confided in us,
especially the autumn before the plane crash.

"*Ke a tti mo a ni a qwi me nwa ne*
ta ma ni i a na ta wi ke e ska wa ni.
I will tell you that I do not like
your intention to travel," his grandmother
had forewarned. "*Ne ta tti ne wa a qwi me ko.*
It bothers me greatly." She had explained
to Fred how she sensed misfortune
through the decomposition of a potato,
how it lingered in the house for days,
that she would not find its source
until the malediction was complete.
In half-delirium and half-sleep I know
of no way to reverse Fred's impermanence.
Certain bones affixed to my limbs
will not transport me to bring him
back. An attempt at The Contrary
would only interfere with a shadow
that continually relives
its preparation for death.

The Handcuff Symbol

We were struggling over a small pearl-
handled Saturday Night Special.
Like three angry adolescents,
so many thousands of miles
from Black Eagle Child,
we were turning an afternoon
college kegger at the Greek Theatre
into a perilous scene:

Weasel Heart, the one who held
the pistol either wanted to shoot
himself or another. A random execution
of someone, nonetheless. We pleaded
first in our language, hoping
such words and their common
sense inflections would subdue
despondency and remind him
of the acquiescent but *living*
grandfathers we represented.
"*Ba ki se na no tta qwi ba
e ya bi me ko ye be te na wa tti.*
Let go of the pistol before you
accidently shoot a bystander."

Like that famous war photograph
of American soldiers raising a flag
over Iwo Jima, we raised the pistol
together and waved it high above
the silhouettes of palm trees —
and it began firing. In the concrete
earth basin, sparks from the hollowpoint
shells flew out from the thin space
between cylinder and barrel.

The red muzzle flash lit
the poverty and mold
of our skeletons.

     / / /

Before the loudspeaker spoke,
the helicopter's spotlight
came through the windows of the log
cabin I was born in. The same greasy
curtains were there, still held
by a stone-smooth yarn string.
Over the woodstove, still unchanged
except for her dilated, opaque pupils,
Sister Theresa was sprinkling commodity
surplus flour into a skillet of watered-
down pork and beans. She was mouthing
the Spectre's command: "Surrender
yourself to piety." She then
pointed to the dried blood
I had slept on and said,
"Ke ta be qwe tti mo ne ma.
Your pillow." As I gently
touched my face for wounds,
I found a marble floating
under the skin of my right wrist.
That's when a tribal committee
member, who was acting as liason
on behalf of the authorities,
knocked on the partially-open door.
I could see the shadow of his fat body
breathing nervously on the bright floor.
"The family of the injured party
is out there also. So there's
witnesses."

/ / /

I couldn't remember a damn thing
except the final humiliating moment
in being where we were, what we were about
to do. There's nothing more disgraceful
than Indians in serious trouble —
in faraway places. How we are able
to travel and meet has to be nomadic
instinct. Truth aside, we often react
like beached whales, and this culture
keeps throwing us back into the black,
chaotic sea. Although we thrash about
for our lives, however demented and painful
it has been, we drown others in the process.

/ / /

I am simply relating this dream
as preface to my belief they often
reoccur in reality. Sometimes in reverse.
The handcuffs, for instance, were positive.
Yet I can imagine the power of a crying
family — relatives of whoever we shot.
Point is, the next night after this dream,
a police officer actually wrapped
my bleeding palms and wrist with gauze,
and he radioed an ambulance for me.
And the gunshots? They turned out
to be my palms busting through
the hot windows of a burning
but empty house. Small caliber
gunfire can sound like glass
being broken. And the marble
under my wrist was in actuality

a hematoma or blood clotting.
But the drunk who I thought
was in the burning house asked me
for no apparent reason if I still
possessed the pistol. Instead
of being stunned by yet another
correlation, I lied and purposely
implanted a continuing vision
of this evil piece in his mind.
I could have bled to death
were it not for the gauze cuffs.

The Dream of Purple Birds
in Marshall, Washington

My people back home love purple —
on clothes for ceremonial or everyday wear.
But the two birds who reside near the city
of Spokane, like us, wear this color as well.
On morning two, they flutter and tap
their purple bodies against our window.
They attempt to tell us something.
Or as I dread, as I have felt
through sleepnessness,
they are the once-life of two women
whose body parts lie scattered
and hidden safely under the dirt and rocks
of a railroad track —
the same one that winds through
this community, this pinetree-lined
valley. In desperation I ask one bird,
"*Ka shi ya bi ke te sha wi?*
What's the matter with you?"
With its purple mask and cape, the bird
hopped on a branch and turned more towards
my way as further testament:
the underside of its body was white-colored
with red speckled lines flowing from its neck
to its chest. These innocent ladies are here
somewhere, they tell me, beckoning you
from dream, from Iowa, from yourself.
Tonight, to keep all this away from me,
I will apply a thin, transparent coat
of yellow paint over the top half
of my round face: *I refuse to be*
their spiritual conduit and release
in a valley where the sun darkens early,
in a valley where a large, red fluorescent
cross is physically so much stronger
than I . . .

Two Poems for Southeastern Washington

Steptoe Butte reigns in the moonlit clouds
over Palouse country. And they call this structure
a butte? Back home, if this rose up from the flat
farmlands it would be deemed a *Mountain that was God*.
High above is Bullchild's celestial pursuer:
Moonwoman rests her body and leg
on a communication tower.
The supernatural history
of Stars.

/ / /

Eight-wheeled tractors — not the ones
we are accustomed to seeing in Iowa —
roll over the steepest hills
with precision without the slightest
threat of tipping over. Even if they
were upside-down they would not falter
because of their even proportion
over the undulating earth. (Think
of all the farmer's lives that could
be saved by these gravity-wise machines.)
Though I have nothing to do with agriculture,
I am astounded. More so, when the giant tractors
dive, reappear and dive earthward
over the landscape, swimming
like muskrats with serious intent.

Fox Guides From La Crosse On

She summoned
Fox-allies in her sleep,
and they surfaced
from roadsides and cliffs —
unafraid and concerned —
to take turns
running in front
of the Toyota
before jumping back
on the assurance
she was taken
care of.

Upon her waking
at the gas station
in Decorah, we apprised her
of the multiple appearances
on the detour where we got lost,
how in the moon's new place
they acted like guides.

Unimpressed by our story,
she said, "A *qwi ya to ki*
ta qwa o ne qwe. Hide *ta ta ki;*
Ne shi ya ki te me qwe.
Why did you not run them over.
For the hide; perhaps it's expensive."

Trying once more to emphasize
their importance, we say:
"A *qwi ma ma ni a bi tti ta so wi*
ne o tte ni wa ko sha a ki all year.
Not this many Fox are seen all year."

But it was no use.
She knew we never picked up
animal carcasses on trips.
It just wasn't our way,
especially to first sight
then kill. Our reverence
for her guides
was made unimportant.

"For a purpose," we later
postulated. There is no obvious
explanation to snowdrifts which
avoid the bird-shaped plants
that communicate with her.
Human-sounding voices in
their exhale of green breath . . .

Shadows of Clouds

For Sara Jumping Eagle

From the frosted morning window I look out
at the new yard and make the mistake of thinking
a mound of gray ashes as last traces of winter
in spring. Visually, I believe bark and soot
have melted into the snow.

And then I recall all the brush that was burned
for a week to clear this "alloted tribal acre."

Why must I conjure this tortuous illusion?

When blizzards materialize from His Breath:
half a world, half a world away,
sending stars over the warm
mountain haze. Shadows of clouds
over other clouds.

Mesquakie Love Song

Ke te na,
ke te na wa na,
ne ki wa tti
me to se ne ni

It is true,
It is true then,
I am a lonely
human being.

Ke te na,
ke te na wa na,
ne ki wa tti
me to se ne ni

It is true,
It is true then,
I am a lonely
human being.

Me sko ta ka a i ki
ma a ki to to si wa ki
ne ka ki wa tti me ko ki

Unfortunately, too,
these crickets (and their singing)
make me lonely.

Ke te na,
ke te na wa na,
ne ki wa tti
me to se ne ni

It is true,
It is true then,
I am a lonely
human being.

NOTES

The Significance of a Water Animal — The Mesquakie word, *O ki ma*, can be translated into English as The Sacred Chief. According to my grandmother, Ada K. Old Bear, before we — the Mesquakie or Red Earth People — were sculpted from the earth, there was *O ki ma*: a human being who came from the very flesh and blood of Creator's heart; a divine decision-maker whose sole purpose in life was and is to guide us through the expanse created. My grandmother's sons, Charles and David Old Bear, are the traditional Chiefs of the Mesquakie Tribe. In 1856, their great-grandfather, *Ma mi nwa ni ke*, initiated the historic purchase and establishment of our tribal homeland in Central Iowa. Akin to the ethereal history of the *O ki ma*, the Water Animal, Muskrat or "Earth-diver" is an integral part of earth's beginnings.

The Language of Weather — It is said that whirlwinds whether comprised of dust, leaves or snow represent the eternally trapped shadows or "souls" of the deceased who have yet to be transferred ceremonially to the Here-after and replaced by another (living person) via the Adoption Ceremony. If this ceremony isn't performed, the forgotten shadow turns into a whirlwind — or even a nocturnal bird of prey.

The King Cobra as Political Assassin — Shortly before the attempted Presidential assassination in 1981, I had a graphic dream about fighting serpents. For creative purposes I associated the serpents to the would-be assassin and the holder of the highest office in this country. As information gradually surfaced about the alleged influences of the movie "Taxi Driver" upon these events, I imagined being prescient. In the end, however, my dream was far from Hollywood's portrayal of a demented cabbie, sleazy city life and politics. The truth was, I was captivated by a strip of wilderness outside of the Settlement's borders where eagles actually stopped to rest and hunt. I once contemplated its acquisition.

The First Dimension of Skunk — One part of this poem is taken from a story entitled "Confessing Poverty to a Supernatural Strobelight." While one isn't usually required to state what is true or not, I am compelled by memory — and perhaps respect — to acknowledge the three owls, who, on one autumn night in 1980, collectively or individually, manifested themselves as a series of bizarre, transforming lights. Grace Mad Soldier and Alfred Pretty Boy-in-the-Woods offered the following possibilities on what the lights could have been: 1.) apprentices of sorcery who sought to drive us away from the isolated river bottom; 2.) ghosts from an old village which was located near our residence; 3.) the shadows or "souls" of the deceased who have not been accorded the Adoption Ceremony; 4.) a malignant, floating disease in search of a human host. For the miraculous display of flying lights we will always remember, including their mass exodus several nights later, we thought the fifth possibility was extraterrestials. In such manifestations, however, inexplicability is a perfect mask.

Eagle Crossing, July 1975 — Composed largely from fiction but influenced in part by fragmented readings on the Blackfeet, this work is one of the eleven poems in this collection based on experimentation. Linguistically, the Mesquakie translation of the English name "Big Foot"is *Me ma ke ka ta ta* or Big Footed One, which is remarkably identical to the Blackfeet pronunciation and definition of the same name. Source: Mr. Floyd Rider, Two Medicine Lake Singers, East Glacier Park, Montana.

All Star's Thanksgiving — In November of 1965, I attended a dusk to dawn gathering where *amanita* — a mushroom with hallucinogenic properties — was ingested for religious purposes. Sensing my interest, my grandmother who was the congregation's cook at the time, encouraged further attendance. I made three visits in all before spiritual curiousity exhausted my immature mind. The songs and prayers which addressed alcoholism, extreme poverty and social repression were too vivid. To see this in my youth made me realize what the tribe had to contend with. I respected the Well-Off Man Congregation's ways but chose not to go back. To my grandmother, this was one part of the four religions in her life. She possesses an extraordinary gift for understanding other people's beliefs. But the foundation for all this is the Principal Mesquakie Belief.

The Dream of Purple Birds in Marshall, Washington — In the spring of 1987, upon our arrival at Eastern Washington University near Spokane to begin a teaching residency, Stella and I were driven by our hosts to a small community where we were to stay. As we began to descend into this picturesque valley, there was a ceaseless, disturbing feeling I had somehow visited the area before. I experienced a déjà vu of sorts, but this particular one stayed until I realized through dream or reincarnation that I had once witnessed the brutal homicide of two white women by two white men.

For several days, we were also puzzled by two birds who came to the kitchen window every morning to hover and peck at what must have been their reflections. Out of this situation, including the insomnia caused by a dormitory cot, I concluded hypothetically that the birds were the "souls" of the two white women who I truly felt were buried *somewhere* along the railroad tracks south of Marshall. If they were indeed "around" I felt their salvation depended not on me but on the forty-foot high cross whose neon tubes of red towered over the quiet, unsuspecting community every night.

A *Drive to Lone Ranger & Race of the Kingfishers* —

> "In the gradual darkness our conversation centers on Northern Lights: celestial messengers in green atomic oxygen, highlighted by red — the color of our impending nuclear demise."

> "Their purpose is to apprise us of the Aurora Borealis, and how such lights will bring the true end."

One Mesquakie prophecy warns when the Northern Lights reach across the skies and touch the southern horizon, a great world war will ensue, causing an end to all life.

In two imaginary situations — the final "Flag War" and "Nuclear Winter" — I incorporate this omen.

/ / /

> "As fiery sparks begin to materialize on an overturned skillet, the caterpillars stop."

This "sparks" theme is taken from childhood when Louise Stabs-me-in-the-Back, my aunt, used to prepare *be ko te*, biscuit, for the family. I would kneel beside the fire and wait anxiously until the cooking was done. Louise would turn the skillet over, knowing I would watch in fascination as sparks crisscrossed the hot skillet's surface. "Somewhere right now," she would say, "there must be a war." In my mind I saw brave "spark" soldiers come out in the raging battle to drag away their wounded comrades.

The First Dimension of Skunk, Nothing Could Take Away the Bear-King's Image, & A Woman's Name is in the Second Verse — "Claremont," "San Gabriel Mountains," "Orozco's murals in Frary Hall," and "Smiley Hall," are places and recollections taken from two academic years at Pomona College in Southern California where this Journey of Words began.

Two Poems for Southeastern Washington — "Bullchild" and "Moonwoman" is in reference to the late Percy Bullchild's story of pre-Blackfeet origins found in *The Sun Came Down*, Harper & Row. To avenge the death of her secret lover — Snakeman — Moonwoman is forever in pursuit of Creator Sun and their seven sons, The Big Dipper.

Emily Dickinson, Bismarck and the Roadrunner's Inquiry — "I would be out of place in the tundra or desert, hunting moose for its meat and hide, tracking roadrunners for their feathers" is in reference to the Algonquin-speaking tribes of Canada and Northeastern Mexico. Variations of the Algonquin language are spoken on the North American continent by the Cree, Blackfeet, Chippewa, Kickapoo, Mexican-Kickapoo, Sauk, and Mesquakie Tribes — to name a few.

Mesquakie Tribal Celebration Songs — These traditional songs are included in a February 27, 1987 audio recording of the Woodland Drum Group produced by Canyon Records, 1411 N. 16th, Phoenix, AZ 85430. The singers, including Stella and I, are from the Mesquakie (Red Earth) Tribal Settlement of Central Iowa.

Acknowledgement is made to the editors of the following publications in which some of these poems first appeared:

AKWEKON:
    Debut of the Woodland Drum
AKWESASNE NOTES:
    The Significance of a Water Animal
    All Star's Thanksgiving
    The Language of Weather
AMERICAN POETRY REVIEW:
    From the Spotted Night
    The First Dimension of Skunk
AMICUS JOURNAL:
    My Grandmother's Words (and Mine) on the Last
        Spring Blizzard
ANOTHER CHICAGO MAGAZINE:
    Three Translated Poems for October
BLOOMSBURY REVIEW:
    Green Threatening Clouds
CALIBAN:
    The Dream of Purple Birds in Marshall, WA
CHARITON REVIEW:
    If the Word for Whale is Right
GREENFIELD REVIEW:
    Eagle Crossing, July 1975
LUNA TACK:
    Three Views of a Northern Pike
MANHATTAN POETRY REVIEW:
    The Personification of a Name
NEW YORK QUARTERLY:
    Fred Bloodclot Red's Composition
NORTH DAKOTA QUARTERLY:
    Emily Dickinson, Bismarck, and the Roadrunner's Inquiry
NORTHWEST REVIEW:
    A Drive to Lone Ranger

PRACTICES OF THE WIND:
   Fox Guides From LaCrosse On
   Shadows of Clouds
   Two Poems for Southeastern Washington
SONORA REVIEW:
   Always is He Criticized
SULFUR:
   Nothing Could Take Away the Bear-King's Image
TAOS REVIEW:
   The Suit of a Hand
   The Black Antelope Tine
THE CLOUDS THREW THIS LIGHT:
   Nineteen Eighty Three
TRI-QUARTERLY:
   Wa ta se Na ka mo ni, Viet Nam Memorial
TYUONYI:
   Race of the Kingfishers
UNIVERSITY OF PORTLAND REVIEW:
   Cool Places of Transformation
VIRGINIA QUARTERLY REVIEW:
   A Woman's Name is in the Second Verse
   The Handcuff Symbol
WICAZO SA REVIEW:
   Colleen's Faith
WILLOW SPRINGS:
   Quail and His Role in Agriculture
WOOSTER REVIEW:
   Journal Entry, November 12, 1960
   Mesquakie Love Song #1, #2, #3

Ray A. Young Bear is a lifetime resident of the Mesquakie (Red Earth) Tribal Settlement, which is located near the rural community of Tama in Central Iowa. For the past eighteen years, he has been a frequent contributor to the field and study of contemporary Native American poetry. His poems have appeared in numerous anthologies and magazines, including *American Poetry Review, Sulfur, Tri-Quarterly, Shaking the Pumpkin, An Introduction to Poetry* and *Harper's Anthology of 20th Century Native American Poetry*. His first book of poems, *Winter of the Salamander,* was published by Harper & Row. Young Bear has taught at the Institute of American Indian Arts, Eastern Washington University and The University of Iowa. Along with his spouse, Stella, he is also a singer and co-founder of the Woodland Song & Dance Troupe of Arts Midwest, a nine state performing arts program. Young Bear is currently at work on *Stories from the Woodland Region* (non-fiction), *The Rock Island Hiking Club* (poems) and *Black Eagle Child Reserve* (fiction).

$3/00^2$

$2\ 9/94$